The Vocation
of the Catholic
University Professor

UNIVERSITY
of MARY PRESS

Published in the United States of America
by University of Mary Press
7500 University Drive
Bismarck, ND 58504
www.umary.edu

ISBN: 978-0-9988728-7-2

Nihil Obstat & Imprimatur

✝ The Most Reverend David D. Kagan, D.D., P.A., J.C.L
Bishop of Bismarck
28 January 2020

The *Nihil Obstat* and *Imprimatur* are official declarations
that a book or pamphlet is free of doctrinal or moral error.
No implication is contained therein that those who granted
them agree with the content or statements expressed.

Design: Jerry Anderson

Printed in Canada

Preface

Education is simply the soul of a society
as it passes from one generation to another.

— G.K. CHESTERTON

IN THE SUMMER of 2017, Dr. Christopher Blum of the Augustine Institute offered a series of superb retreat conferences for University of Mary professors gathered in prayer at St. John's Abbey, Collegeville.[1] I was able on that occasion to be a retreatant with my faculty, and it was a beautiful experience of grace and healing.

Yes, the Lord had something in mind also for an administrator like me during those languid June days in rural Minnesota.

Gently but steadily, in the courteous manner of God's grace, I was brought to see that a kind of quiet resentment had been building in me over the course of nearly ten years in my role at the university. While the faculty were reading great literature with our students and accompanying them on adventures of scientific discovery and philosophic wonder, the daily energies of my heart

---

[1] *Christ, the Wisdom of God: Retreat Conferences for the Faculty of the University of Mary* (Bismarck: University of Mary Press, 2017).

were consumed by more reptilian tasks: budgets, accreditation, snow removal. As the growth of the university and a deliberate economy in administrative staffing lengthened my days with more work and worry, I was confounded by requests for course releases from young, energetic faculty in their second or third year of teaching. And earnest, non-evil policy reforms to serve the common good and secure a viable future for the university were often enough met with murmuring or criticism that impressed me as all at once exquisite in expression, self-contradictory, and impractical.

But praying with and for the faculty in a sustained way over several days caused a new tenderness to wash over me and renewed in me a conviction I had felt so strongly when I first came to the University of Mary: that it is a remarkable privilege to serve professors, to care for their needs, to provide space and support so they can do well the real work of the university — educating students.

A Catholic university should invite students into a community of profound intellectual conversion. Its atmosphere is alive with the *gaudium de veritate* of Saint Augustine, 'the joy in the truth.' Just there, in a classroom or laboratory at the end of the hallway, is to be found the "stupor" or astonishment of mind of Dante's *Convivio*. There are many ways for this conversion to happen, but it simply will not happen without the teaching faculty. They are the lifeblood.

Nemo dat quod non habet. 'No one gives what he does not have.' If a Christian community is to foster intellectual conversion, it must itself be characterized by continuous, humble, joyful repentance. This means the professors, and also those who serve them.

And so a set of pressing questions pierced my heart: Was I steadily repenting of all envy and self-pity? Was I *with* my own faculty in the trenches of their hearts, recalling with them the lofty ideals of our shared vocation in education which is, after all, a matter of the life and death of souls? Was I doing enough to summon them beyond the frontiers of excellence or efficiency to genuine holiness?

The Lord reminded me during that retreat how hard it is even for the good-hearted disciple to maintain such a stance of repentance. And the calling to teach at a Catholic university is both inherently noble and crucially important, so we should fully expect the corresponding temptations and dangers to be stern.

Thus began a series of conversations with my spiritual director and some close confidants about whether it could be helpful to sketch out a fuller vision for truly teaching at a place like the University of Mary. The resulting essay has been a collaborative effort of "back and forth," and I hasten to add that it already reflects much of what happens at Mary when we are at our best.

It also reflects, I should admit, the substance of what I pray for in my specific office of priestly intercession for the academic community entrusted to my care. I am therefore hoping that its publication will tangibly remind me to keep repenting and — with a joyful, thankful heart — thus to pray without ceasing (1 Thes 5:16-18).

Monsignor James Shea, President
The University of Mary

28 January 2020
The Feast of Saint Thomas Aquinas,
Doctor of the Church,
Patron of Students and Universities

Table of Contents

Introduction

1. Christians know that every walk of life comes with a voca-
    tional dimension. The simplest and humblest tasks can
    be opportunities to honor God, to bring his presence to
    others, and to contribute, at least indirectly, to building the
    Kingdom. For the one called to be a university professor,
    that vocational dimension is intensified. The professor
    at a Catholic university is involved in the pursuit and
    dissemination of truth, and beyond this, the professor is
    called to care for immortal souls, to help in the formation of
    minds and spirits after the image of Christ. This means that
    the professor accepts an important trust, one that bears an
    explicit apostolic charge. Christian educators are builders of
    the Kingdom in a direct and momentous way.

2. The vocational importance of the educator can be seen in
    the traditional instinct and practice of the Church to entrust
    education, especially at the highest levels, to individuals or
    communities explicitly consecrated to the service of God.
    We need not see in that long practice the only possible
    arrangement; in fact, given the important mission of the
    laity in witnessing to Christ in a society structured like
    ours, it may not even be the best arrangement. Nevertheless,

it underlines for us the nature of the educator's task as an apostolic charge. Those who take up university teaching, whether lay or consecrated, should be aware that they have chosen more than a profession or career path that can be pursued according to the logic of professional advancement and personal development alone. They have signed onto a mission and embraced a high calling, a calling that brings with it a specific set of loyalties and responsibilities.

3. This essay is an attempt to describe the heart of the Christian professor's vocation, an especially urgent task in our day when university teaching has taken its place beside other secular professions, and when universities, including many Catholic universities, are having difficulty remembering the true nature of their intellectual apostolate. What is discussed here is not meant to be an exhaustive account of the professorial vocation nor the final word on how that vocation should be lived. Its aims are more limited. It hopes to bring to the fore certain aspects of the Catholic university's purpose and the professor's role in that purpose that are often overlooked, in the hope of sparking further discussion about the nature of this important Christian call.

I

The Dual Vocation of the Catholic University

4. There are two aspects of the vocation of the university professor, related but distinct, that are worth examining separately. One is the imperative to seek, guard, and communicate truth; the second is the responsibility to care for the young immortal souls who have been entrusted to the university.[2] Putting it this way is not meant as a reformulation of the often-discussed question of teaching versus research or of how the two may rightly be combined in a university setting. Apart from any determination about whether or how much a given institution should be a center of research, these two aspects of the Catholic university or college's vocation remain paramount.

5. As to the first of these, the call to honor and pursue truth: In a significant historical development, when early Christianity made its way into the cultures of the ancient world, it came to understand itself not as a further development of that world's *religions* (apart of course from the Jewish religion) but as the fulfillment of its *philosophical* schools. Early Christian apologists and theologians such as Justin Martyr, Origen, and

---

[2] *Ex Corde Ecclesiae*, Par. 4: "It is the honour and responsibility of a Catholic University to consecrate itself without reserve to the cause of truth."

Clement of Alexandria spoke of themselves as philosophers and identified Christianity as the "true philosophy." Here is how Justin described his conversion, an event that took place around A.D. 130: "A fire was suddenly kindled in my soul. I fell in love with the prophets and these men who had loved Christ; I reflected on all their words and found that this philosophy alone was true and profitable. That is how and why I became a philosopher. And I wish that everyone felt the same way that I do." The Church Fathers sought to correct whatever errors or imbalances they found in the ancient philosophies, whether Platonic, Stoic, or Aristotelian, but they admired much of what they found there and built upon those insights.

6. Under the long tutelage of Christianity and Judaism before it, we have become used to the idea that the practice of religion leads naturally to an understanding of the cosmos and to an ordered moral life. But before Christianity, most of the world's religions had not been interested in an overall account of truth or in a particular moral posture. They were geared to placating the gods and to invoking and participating in the rhythms of nature, which often involved rites and ecstatic states in which rational thinking was purposely set aside. In contrast to this, the Greek philosophical quest for the *logos*, for reason, order, rationality, or the word, as it is variously translated, was an attempt to master the whole of reality in all its interlocking parts. Socrates was accused by his opponents of being an atheist, but he was not at all an irreligious thinker. He was interested in the whole of reality, natural and supernatural, and he found the contemporary myths of the gods to be either silly or immoral. Interestingly, the same accusation of atheism was lodged against early Christians, and for many

of the same reasons. Christians had little use for pagan myths and the worship of the gods and either attacked or ignored the religions of their time. But the philosophic quest for truth, the desire to grasp hold of all that was real, was incorporated even into the Christian scriptures, where the second person of the Trinity through whom the world was created bore the name of "reason." The heart of the Christian religion is thus an account of reality. "For this I was born, and for this I have come into the world, to bear witness to the truth. Everyone who is of the truth hears my voice" (Jn 18:37). When Jesus spoke these words to Pilate at his trial, Pilate responded, perhaps cynically, with a rhetorical question that could stand for much of the modern secular university's quandary: "What is truth?"

7. The Christian embrace of the Greek philosophical tradition, a pattern that had already been underway among the Jews, was a momentous event in the history of world religions.[3] For our purposes it is important to note that it had this consequence: that anyone who was attempting to be a devout Christian would by necessity be pursuing the totality of what was real. Christianity meant not just the performance of certain rites or sacrifices, nor the pursuit of ecstatic consciousness-altering states, nor even merely the adherence to a given moral stance; it meant the embrace of the whole truth about God and creation. The "renewal of the mind"

[3] Pope Benedict XVI expressed this point in his address to the University of Regensburg in 2006, "Faith, Reason and the University": "The encounter between the Biblical message and Greek thought did not happen by chance. The vision of Saint Paul, who saw the roads to Asia barred and in a dream saw a Macedonian Man plead with him: 'Come over to Macedonia and help us!' (cf. Acts 16:6-10) — this vision can be interpreted as a 'distillation' of the intrinsic necessity of a rapprochement between Biblical faith and Greek inquiry."

(Rom 12:1) was the goal of every Christian, even of those who were not formally educated. It was at the heart of what it meant to be converted to Christ.

8. This renewal of the mind by the embrace of truth in its multiform expressions, incumbent upon all Christians by virtue of their faith, was ever the special hallmark of the university, the Christian institution where that pursuit finds its most complete and intensive expression. The Catholic university is thus interested in everything, in all that exists, in the whole of reality, not simply as disjointed collections of information but as aspects of a cosmos, facets of a united whole that can be sought and grasped by the human mind and spirit: the being and nature of God, the visible and the invisible worlds, humans in their individuality and in their social relations, ethics and the moral life, and the way all these interrelate in the formation of the human mind and will. When Harvard University took as its motto *Veritas Christo et Ecclesiae,* and Yale, similarly, *Lux et Veritas,* they were pointing to this fundamental charge of the Christian university. Truth — reality — is the measure of the university's task, the end to which it constantly returns. If the university loses its grasp on reality, it fails in its purpose and becomes either useless or dangerous to those who inhabit it.[4]

---

[4] Consider this passage from Pope John XXIII's encyclical *Ad Petri Cathedram* (1959): "All the evils which poison men and nations and trouble so many hearts have a single cause and a single source: ignorance of the truth — and at times even more than ignorance, a contempt for truth and a reckless rejection of it. Thus arise all manner of errors, which enter the recesses of men's hearts and the bloodstream of human society as would a plague. These errors turn everything upside down: they menace individuals and society itself" (Par. 6)… "How can God, who is truth, approve or tolerate the indifference, neglect, and sloth of those who attach no importance to matters on which our eternal salvation depends; who attach no importance to pursuit and attainment of necessary truths, or to the offering of that proper worship which is owed to God alone?" (Par. 18).

9. "If you continue in my word, you are truly my disciples, and you will know the truth, and the truth will make you free" (Jn 8:31-2). These words of Jesus point to yet another reason why the call to truth is so important, and they lead us to the second aspect of the Catholic professor's vocation. According to the Christian account of things, knowledge of the truth and the determination to live by that knowledge sets the human spirit free. Truth is what we were created for, and possession of the truth will save us. For Christians, truth is not just an assemblage of facts about the world. Truth is embodied in a person, and it is ultimately gained through knowledge of that person: Jesus said of himself, "I am the way, the truth, and the life" (Jn 14:6). Because so much is at stake for each individual in this question of truth, the call to pursue truth also involves the care of those who are seeking that same reality. To be stewards of truth for others demands charity as a motivating principle — the loving concern to see others gain the truth and so be set free. This charity becomes especially important for those serving the young, who are still in the process of laying the foundations of their minds and characters and are therefore uniquely open to truth with all its demands and possibilities, but who are also more vulnerable to malformations that can make the embrace of truth difficult.

10. In light of the university's vocational task, it is not surprising that early universities were largely put into the hands of religious communities whose pattern of life provided, first, the practical freeing up of time and energy for the contemplation of truth (a pattern that had already been established in the ancient world, as for example in Plato's Academy and in the Lyceum of Aristotle), and second, an

explicit commitment to charity in the care of the young. As modern universities have lost the sense of their true vocation, the position of the university professor has increasingly come to be seen simply as a job choice, a path for career advancement whose qualifications have little to do with the inner disposition of the professor toward love of truth and love of students. Hence the intellectual and moral crisis faced by modern secular academia is hardly surprising.

II

Philosophies of Education

---

11. It is a necessary aspect of any educational scheme, program, or technique that it is founded on a set of philosophical assumptions about human nature. In order to say anything of substance about teaching or training humans, we need an understanding of what a well-formed human looks like, what makes for a good human society, and what the necessary attainments are to make progress toward those personal and communal goals. Once we get beyond the simplest kinds of teaching — like showing someone how to tie a shoe — we are forced to make assumptions about the nature of the human and the kind of world we inhabit. We often don't think explicitly about such assumptions in the midst of our teaching and scholarly duties, but this does not mean that the assumptions are not present; it only means that they have become accepted and internalized by the educational culture we inhabit.

12. Because any given educational program demands a specific theory of what a good human looks like — an anthropology — and because any given anthropology can only be articulated in the context of an overall understanding of the universe — the meaning of life and the purpose of human

activity — every educational program is ultimately founded on a particular philosophical, even theological, understanding of the world. Whether we conceive that there is or is not a God, whether God has or has not revealed something about himself and his creation, whether he has made demands upon those he has created, what promises or hopes he has offered, whether there is an order proper to human relations and human behavior founded in the nature of things; such questions and others like them cannot be avoided in articulating an educational scheme. Our answers to them will affect all aspects of our educational practice from the outset. There has never been, nor can there be in the nature of things, a philosophically or theologically — and therefore morally — "neutral" educational program. This is true of the technical and professional disciplines as well as of the arts and humanities. The simple decision to take time and energy to teach a given subject or skill — along with the need to sort out the inevitable ethical questions that consistently arise in the application of that subject or skill — implies a judgment about its importance and its purpose rooted in an anthropology and a social philosophy.[5]

13. When a society or culture is in general agreement about its religious and philosophical foundations and therefore

---

[5] *Ex Corde Ecclesiae*, par. 18: "Because knowledge is meant to serve the human person, research in a Catholic University is always carried out with a concern for the ethical and moral implications both of its methods and of its discoveries. This concern, while it must be present in all research, is particularly important in the areas of science and technology. It is essential that we be convinced of the priority of the ethical over the technical, of the primacy of the person over things, of the superiority of the spirit over matter. The cause of the human person will only be served if knowledge is joined to conscience. Men and women of science will truly aid humanity only if they preserve 'the sense of the transcendence of the human person over the world and of God over the human person.'"

its anthropology — its understanding of human nature — educational conflicts tend to be limited, usually dealing with differing emphases or the value of different methods to reach more or less agreed-upon ends. But when a culture or a society is in conflict about basic anthropological questions, educational differences become sharper and more significant. In such times it is important to be clear about the philosophical and theological presuppositions behind differing educational visions. We are living in such a time of conflicting anthropologies. It is therefore important for all serious educators, and especially Christian and Catholic ones, to take thought for the assumptions that lie behind their educational policies and practices and for the resulting coherence (or incoherence) of their educational institutions. To this end, it can be helpful to consider some of the historical background to our present circumstances.

III

The Historical Context

14. As is well known, the university arose as an educational institution in medieval Europe. This is not an accidental detail in the effort to understand universities, because no educational institution stands apart from the society that gave it birth and the assumptions that underlay that society's view of reality. The medievals had been heirs to a long educational tradition going back to the Greeks. Through an involved process lasting many centuries, the Church sifted the educational practices of the ancient world, embracing much of the Greek ideal and giving it a new and deeper life by undergirding it with a Christian metaphysics. The medieval university was a natural expression of a Christian understanding of things, arising from the idea of a God who transcended the world, who created the world with a clear purpose, who expressed himself most fully in the *logos,* in rationality and order, and who fashioned humanity in His own image to participate in his life. Such a view conferred a tone of seriousness about life in general and especially about the life of the mind. The implications of these fundamental principles of faith were seen in every aspect of the medieval university's life, from the ordering of its studies to the care of its students.

15. Over the centuries the Church developed a rich intellectual tradition founded on what were understood to be the twin sources of genuine knowledge: truths discovered by human reason and truths revealed by God and grasped through faith.[6] At the university, the ordering of the mind was wrought out and passed on to a rising generation. As such, the medieval university emerged as one of the three key institutions by which Christendom expressed its quest for coherence and unity. Around the *Papacy* was ordered the world of faith; around the *Empire* the concern for temporal governance; and around the *University* the life of the mind. An example of the university's cultural importance can be seen in the fourteenth century crisis of a divided papacy. When Europe's political order was separated into opposing camps in support of two (and for a time three) different popes, such that the fundamental unity of Christendom was in jeopardy, Christian society turned to its third source of unity, and a way to heal the divisions was found through the universities. It is hard to imagine contemporary universities bearing that kind of cultural and social influence.

16. A great change in the understanding of humanity began to grip the European mind during the latter part of the seventeenth century. At first involving only a small number of educated people, this new way of thinking increasingly dominated the upper classes and broke violently upon the social and political life of Europe at the time of the French Revolution. The new revolutionary ideas were philosophical

---

[6] Thomas Aquinas, *Summa Contra Gentiles*, Ch.3, par. 2: "There is a twofold mode of truth in what we profess about God. Some truths about God exceed all the ability of the human reason... but there are some truths which the natural reason also is able to reach."

and anthropological as well as political, and so they necessarily gave rise to new schemes of education.

17. The change made itself felt institutionally wherever the new anthropology triumphed. In France, the Christian universities were forcibly shut down (1794) and new ones were founded on a different basis. (The French have always had a penchant for the clarity of the guillotine.) In Germany, the process was less abrupt but ultimately no less decisive: The University of Berlin (1811) represented the vanguard of a new anthropology and a new theology. In England, the University of London (1826) was established by Enlightenment philosopher Jeremy Bentham to express the new educational ideals. In the United States, the University of Virginia (1818) was founded by Thomas Jefferson with the same goal. These institutions continued to call themselves universities and carried on many of the functions and even many of the traditions of the Christian universities that preceded them. But because they were rooted in a different philosophy or set of philosophies, they went at their task in momentously different ways. This led to the emergence of two fundamentally different kinds of universities, each founded on a particular set of assumed *a priori* principles concerning the nature of humans and the best way to achieve human salvation and progress. This way of putting things, while true in an ideal-typical sense, does not mean that those who ran and worked in the universities immediately perceived the choices they were making as enactment of such principles. In the midst of the philosophical confusion of the last two centuries, many universities have maintained themselves at some level of intellectual incoherence, forging an uneasy alloy of Christian

and secular Enlightenment ideas. But institutions tend to consistency over time, as their essential principles work themselves out through the generations.

18. Important as the university was to Christian society, it continued to be a vital social institution for those pursuing an Enlightenment ideal, in theory perhaps even more important than it had been for Christendom. In the emerging enlightened world, the human race would be saved not by repentance and faith in God but by the application of knowledge to the problems of the world. Knowledge being the instrument that would further human progress toward perfection, universities were the obvious institutions in which to carry on that saving work. Secular universities thus took on the social significance of what church bodies were for Christendom. Professors, purveyors of a new gospel, were the new clergy; initiation into knowledge was the new baptism that would renew humanity; and the PhD — original research that would conquer yet more knowledge for curing the world's ills — became the new qualification for the role of mankind's benefactor.

19. Currently, most of the institutions of higher education in the West have abandoned their Christian basis, along with their Christian intellectual vocation, and have embraced some version (usually partial and fragmentary) of Enlightenment dogma. Protestant colleges and universities in the United States largely underwent this shift during the late nineteenth and early twentieth centuries. Catholic universities got into the act during the second half of the twentieth century. As the anthropological bases of the society grew ever more confused, universities ceased to

be united by any integrated educational philosophy and could no longer embody or offer to students an overall understanding of reality. They therefore seriously reduced their aspirations, and they instead increasingly sought their institutional unity as businesses that offered technical training and provided certain social and career advantages for their students. Many inside and outside the academy have rightly decried the rampant bureaucratic growth and accompanying cost of the managerial and administrative aspects of the modern university, in which students are viewed simply as consumers whose tastes and desires are to be catered to for the sake of gaining their cash, while faculty are relegated to the margins of the university's concerns except insofar as they further or impede its progress as a successful business. But in the absence of a clear ruling philosophical vision, some such development was inevitable. This modern type of university has become so dominant as to be thought the only one possible, even among many Christians. Most Catholic universities continue to express some concern for the liturgical life of students, and there are often moral themes present (though these can tend to be muddled and insipid), but the specifically intellectual project of the Catholic university, based on Christian first principles, has largely been abandoned.

20. There are many obvious problems with this situation. Here are two. First, in terms of impact on the Church, the disappearance of the Catholic university (as expressed above) has meant that the Church has been left impoverished in its intellectual life and has been made vulnerable to many currents of thought that tend to undermine its fundamental principles. The loss of its universities has also made it diffi-

cult for the Church to pass on its intellectual and cultural heritage to a rising generation of Catholics. Second, as regards the impact of this development on the wider society, the inherent weaknesses of liberal Enlightenment thought concerning God and human nature have had a deleterious effect. In everything but the technical disciplines (conceived in narrowly utilitarian terms), they have left modern secular universities intellectually barren and morally incoherent, the inevitable outworking of a flawed philosophical grounding.

21. We thus face a situation in which both Christian and secular universities are facing a serious crisis: Christian universities because they have forgotten their fundamental principles and secular universities because their anthropological assumptions are inadequate for sustaining serious intellectual activity. By whatever road we may have arrived at this point, it is clear that Catholic institutions of higher learning need a different way forward, a way by which the university is founded on the truths of God, humanity, rationality, and learning provided by a genuinely Christian view of reality. A philosophical and cultural re-founding of our universities is a necessary task and will involve more than simply attempting to go back to an earlier model. It will mean working Christian principles of anthropology and epistemology into the current cultural and educational context, in what will no doubt sometimes be new or reworked institutional forms.

IV

Important Foundational Principles of a Catholic University

---

22. A detailed examination of the differing philosophical assumptions of these two educational institutions, Christian and Enlightenment, would go beyond what is here useful. What follows are three key differences that can provide a kind of shortcut for perceiving the contrast, which in turn might allow questions of a practical nature to arise. These differences of principle involve: (1) the existence and action of God; (2) the proper bases of knowledge; and (3) the doctrine of the Fall.

Concerning the existence and action of God:

23. A Catholic university does not begin with universal doubt, an Enlightenment ideal that is probably impossible to attain even if it were desirable. Rather, the Catholic university arises out of a living organism, the Catholic Church, and assumes as the basis of its intellectual endeavor the truths upon which the Church is founded. The Catholic university starts with the existence of a God who created the universe as an ordered cosmos and who has assigned a special role within that cosmos to humanity. It accepts the doctrines stated by the creeds and set forth in the Sacred Scriptures. These function

as first principles of thought for the university's intellectual project in all its dimensions. When medieval Oxford chose as its motto *Dominus Illuminatio Mea*, 'The Lord is My Light,' the Oxford masters were not engaging in a pious devotional exercise. Rather, they were making clear the principles upon which they were basing their intellectual edifice; they wanted their work to correspond to the truth of things.

24. The Catholic university's insistence on first principles of reason and revelation does not mean that it does not investigate those principles. It works to understand and purify them; it examines them philosophically and theologically; it pursues questions and difficulties that may arise from holding them; and it devises ways of thinking and of ordering knowledge that can aid in an ever better grasp of reality. Beginning with such first principles does not theoretically lead (and has not historically led) to the suffocation of intellectual activity. The reverse is true. Without strong and clear first principles it is impossible to develop traditions of intellectual life that allow a proper development of the mind and a fruitful engagement with the truth of things.

25. Working from its understanding that the world has a Creator who is the source of truth and goodness, the Catholic university has a clear foundation for teaching certain perennial truths. It holds that the world has an inherent meaning beyond the subjective experience of any one individual or of any particular society; it confidently teaches that moral norms expressing goodness and justice are rooted in an unchanging reality transcending all times and cultures,

however much they may need to be translated and brought to life in different cultural contexts; and it asserts that humans are created according to a certain nature and with a specific *telos*, with a meaning and an end in view that originates in the mind of God.

26. The secular university also begins by assuming certain dogmas concerning the existence and action of God in the world. The key secular dogma in this regard might be called functional atheism. Whatever an individual participant in the university's life may think or believe about God or the gods, it is assumed for the university's intellectual mission that God plays no significant role in the operation of the universe or in the ongoing fortunes of the human race. It is important to see that this assumption is the starting point, not the end result, of the secular university's investigations. It is not arrived at scientifically; it is a philosophical point of departure. The practical consequences of such a starting point are many and significant. They are most obviously evident in the biological sciences, the social sciences, and the humanities, but they also set the parameters in subtler ways for the study of the more technical and professional disciplines. Having embraced the principle of functional atheism, the secular university has no basis upon which to build a coherent account of what is good or true — or of what the meaning of life may be — since it has no ground outside the subjective individual or the particular socio-historic context to which it can appeal. As a result, the modern university tends increasingly to engage in limited technical matters that can be experimentally verified and that do not touch on deeper questions of what is good, or what is true, or how a meaningful life is to be lived.

27. Much of the intellectual confusion that so troubles the secular university arises from its odd claim that it makes no *a priori* philosophical assumptions whatsoever. It often distinguishes itself from the Catholic university by insisting that, unlike dogma-bound Catholic institutions, the secular university engages in the "free" pursuit of truth wherever it leads, unshackled by doctrinaire constraints. But there is no ground from which such a supposedly neutral pursuit of truth could possibly take place. The result of this confusion of mind is that secular universities are tied to theological and philosophical assumptions that they either do not recognize or that they deny for the sake of political advantage. By a kind of intrinsic necessity, this state of intellectual incoherence has brought about the unfortunate phenomenon we call "political correctness." Finding that it needs a dogmatic basis for its intellectual project, the secular university instinctively imposes one. But because it insists on its own intellectual disinterestedness and freedom from doctrinaire assumptions, it claims that the dogmas it imposes are self-evident and thereby do not need to be submitted to thoughtful critique. Those reigning assumptions, whether intellectual or moral, are then imposed arbitrarily and coercively. Anyone who demurs from them or challenges them is branded, not as a serious investigator after truth, but as a morally bad or intellectually backward person whose voice should not be heard and who must be run out of the university community. We are thus faced with an ironic phenomenon: The most adamant resistance to open-minded thinking in modern society is found at exactly those institutions claiming such broad-mindedness as their special characteristic. This is not meant to suggest

that secular university professors or administrators are more hypocritical than is usual in people. Rather, it underlines the inadequacy of the conceptions under which they so often labor. Having embraced a dogmatic belief in the ineluctable progress of human cultural and intellectual development and seeing themselves as the standard-bearers of that progressive upward movement, they can hardly help thinking that they are intellectually superior to those who disagree with them — not because they have faced and mastered opposing ideas but because they have an often unexamined faith in the "self-evident" truth of their progressive principles.

Concerning the proper bases of knowledge:

28. As noted earlier, the Catholic university has long understood its intellectual project as founded on two pillars of knowledge, reason and faith, both of which have their origin in God.[7] Reason (which comes by careful and thoughtful inquiry, whether into the natural world or into metaphysical and ethical concepts) and faith (which is revealed to the human race by God) are each genuine sources of truth; and as both coming from God, they are understood to be necessarily complementary rather than contradictory. The Catholic university investigates both, seeking to gain an ever clearer and fuller exercise of rationality and an ever richer and more accurate understanding of revelation. It notes the claims made by each and adjusts each in light of the other,

---

[7] Pope John Paul II's encyclical *Fides et Ratio* (1998) opens with these lines: "Faith and reason are like two wings on which the human spirit rises to the contemplation of truth; and God has placed in the human heart a desire to know the truth—in a word, to know himself—so that, by knowing and loving God, men and women may also come to the fullness of truth about themselves."

such that the reception of the truths of revelation is purified and solidified by reason, and reason is given a sure basis and an understanding of its powers and its limits by faith. Both rationalism — the denial of any of the knowledge that comes from revelation — and fideism — the denial of the knowledge that comes from reason — are rejected by the Catholic university. And while the university begins with the assumption that faith and reason are the twin pillars of knowledge, the validity of that assumption is continually being investigated, and it is given support by its success in bringing about and sustaining an ever broadening intellectual and spiritual tradition.

29. The secular university, in keeping with and deriving from its principle of functional atheism, also begins with an assumption about our sources of knowledge: namely, that the only form of knowledge that can be held as valid is that which is either logically provable or empirically verifiable. This means that both revealed truths of faith and truths arrived at through philosophical and ethical reasoning are relegated to the class of opinions or prejudices. They may be thought charming or consoling to those who hold them, or perhaps distasteful or destructive, but in any case they do not touch upon the intellectual project of the university; they do not deal in genuine knowledge. The embrace of this definition of what can be counted as knowledge — a definition that cannot itself be rationally or empirically proven — has led to a profoundly reduced vision of reality and to a correspondingly shrunken and misshapen scope of the life and business of the university.

Concerning the doctrine of the Fall:

30. The third chapter of the Book of Genesis tells the story of the loss of Eden. That account points to a key Christian understanding about humanity's current plight. The Christian, grieved by the prevalence of both individual and social evil, finds the root of the world's corruption in a moral wound that afflicts all the members of the human race. The core of that disabling moral stance is pride, the human determination to be independent of God and to establish ourselves as the sole arbiters of goodness and truth. Christians have great hope of overcoming the spiritual and intellectual wound of pride, but they recognize that their healing is beyond their own powers. Hence the Christian emphasis on the "good news," the announcement that God has initiated and is bringing about the renewal and revivification of the human race. Christians have been energetic in addressing personal and social evils through the centuries, but they do so with the understanding that fallen human nature is prone to pride and will never be fully restored in this age of time; the ills of the world, rooted as they are in the fallen human mind and spirit, are ultimately insurmountable apart from the action of God.

31. The Enlightenment vision begins with a different foundational doctrine concerning evil. Evil is not the result of an inescapable moral flaw in each individual. People become evil when societal or other circumstantial factors corrupt or harm them. Therefore, the solutions to the world's evils will come as we gain an ever better knowledge of such corrupting external factors and learn to alter their arrangements such that humanity can escape that corruption and grow ever nearer to physical and moral perfection.

32. This difference in understanding has significant consequences. Christians, like the Greeks before them, have held that the heart of all education was moral formation. Whatever the value of acquiring knowledge — and both the Greek and the Christian traditions have put a very high value on it — such knowledge will not bring about anything good unless it is in the hands of the morally good person. To equip the mind without addressing the will was to put dangerous weaponry in the hands of those who had no sense for how or when to use it, who could then unleash great evil on the world. According to the Christian (and Greek) understanding, one could not think properly if one's moral life was in disorder. Hence moral training was an essential aspect of the intellectual project. The secular university, admitting no such moral wound in the individual, has done nothing to address it; it has separated mind and will, viewing the formation of the will as something at least theoretically outside the university's task. One does not have to look very hard to see the seriously negative effects of this mode of education, both on those who undergo it and on the society at large.

❖   ❖   ❖

33. The divergent assumptions about God and humanity noted above, among others, mean that those engaging in the work of university teaching have a clear choice before them concerning what kind of university they hope to sustain: whether it is to be founded on Christian or on secular doctrinal assumptions. The Catholic university can be an intellectually and morally coherent enterprise when it is true to its guiding Christian principles. When it wanders from its core assumptions, however, it quickly loses that

coherence. The secular university is increasingly attempting consistency with its founding dogmas (though it does not call them that), but its assumptions about God and the world are so tenuous and erroneous that it is difficult to mount any consistent account of reality based on them. This explains something of the brittleness and aridity of the secular university's educational vision and its confusion about its task. Professors at a Catholic university need to think with clarity and alertness about their institutions and their profession, lest they slide toward the reigning cultural model and see their work fall into the intellectual and moral confusion and incoherence that has befallen their secular counterparts.

V

Attitudes and Practices to Cultivate

34. It has been noted that teaching at a Catholic university is a career, but it is more; it is a high Christian vocation upon which much depends. As a unique intellectual, pastoral, and apostolic venture, it calls for careful preparation and continued attention to the renewal of the mind, growth in charity, and zeal for God's Kingdom. While university teaching is a source of livelihood, and so necessarily brings with it certain practical issues and constraints that need to be taken into account, these valid concerns need to support rather than subvert the Christian vocation inherent in the teaching profession. In light of our current situation, how might the professor best respond? What sort of attitudes and virtues will help in preparation for the vocation? In short, what are some aspects of the quality of wisdom that is meant to characterize the Christian teacher?[8]

The professor as a servant of truth

35. Universities are gatherings of intellectually gifted people working together to assimilate, increase, and pass on

---

[8] *Ex Corde Ecclesiae*, par. 22: "Christians among the teachers are called to be witnesses and educators of authentic Christian life, which evidences attained integration between faith and life, and between professional competence and Christian wisdom. All teachers are to be inspired by academic ideals and by the principles of an authentically human life."

knowledge. If there has been a besetting temptation for clever people in all times and places, it is intellectual pride: the confidence in one's own powers of thought and action to address and resolve the ills of life. This perennial difficulty has been greatly exacerbated in our current academic culture. Having left behind the idea of original sin along with the practices that had been in place to address its effects, in an unfortunate but inevitable development, the modern secular university has become a hotbed of this kind of intellectual pride. The modern attitude tends to situate pride mainly in relations between humans; we think people are most prideful when they consider themselves in some respect better than others. But Christians have understood pride to refer most centrally to a person's orientation to God. It is possible for thoughtful and courteous people to be lost in profound pride toward God, as they set about "creating" whole universes of meaning and morality — godlike activities — with no reference to that One who is the center of all existence and the source of all meaning and goodness. Christian professors need to be especially on their guard against their own inclinations to intellectual pride and ready to deflect the influence of their environment when it leads in that direction. They will take special concern to cultivate humility of mind and to develop corresponding intellectual habits: such things as understanding the limits of reason, accepting mystery as a necessary aspect of God's revelation, resisting the idea that the world can be cured of its ills by human activity alone, embracing the identity of a created being and rejecting the current culture's attempt to set humans in the place of God, and remembering that intellectual talent is a gift whose purpose is found in service to others rather than in self-aggrandizement.

36. The special antidote to intellectual pride is found in worship. When we worship God rightly, we give ourselves unreservedly to this mysterious Being at the center of all as a sacrificial offering, and we make ourselves available to whatever he might wish to do in and through us. Habitual worship of God rightly situates us amid the cosmos and helps to fashion our identity. More specifically as regards the intellectual vocation, it opens for us the possibility of knowing the truth of things and so is essential for a healthy life of the mind.[9] Furthermore, to worship alongside our students is a tremendous act of wholesome witness and a powerful encouragement and consolation to young minds and hearts.

37. The specialization of university study, to a certain point inevitable and at times necessary, tends to favor a narrow development of mind that works against a quality that John Henry Newman called the highest activity of the intellect: namely, the integration of all that is known toward an understanding of the whole of reality. Professors at a Catholic university will want to find ways to stay interested in everything — in the entirety of things — even while pursuing a specialty. They will want to avoid the blunting effect produced on the mind by the tyranny of specialized knowledge and the tendency it induces toward forgetfulness of the larger meaning of the intellectual venture — the pursuit of truth — which can then trivialize or commodify that noble activity.

---

[9] *Fides et Ratio*, par. 13: "It should be kept in mind that Revelation remains charged with mystery. It is true that Jesus, with his entire life, revealed the countenance of the Father, for he came to teach the secret things of God. But our vision of the face of God is always fragmentary and impaired by the limits of our understanding. Faith alone makes it possible to penetrate the mystery in a way that allows us to understand it coherently."

38. One besetting vice among academics is the tendency to
take up a habitual attitude of hyper-criticism. Both by talent
and by training, academics become adept at the practice of
"critical thinking." If by critical thinking it is meant logical
clarity, care and thoroughness in scholarship, precise use
of language, and sound and fair judgment, then of course
it is a good and even necessary quality for professors. But
too often the critical attitude goes in a different direction
and becomes an optic by which one deals with all of life.
Modern academics are taught to begin with universal doubt,
to question everything, and to submit whatever they deal
with to a searching process of analysis and dismemberment.
Hidden in this kind of critical thinking is an illusory stance
of supposed distance and objectivity from whatever is being
studied. Forgetting that all knowledge begins with the act
of entrusting oneself to an intellectual tradition and working
within it, just as all true friendships begin with entrusting
oneself to another person or community, those who practice
hyper-critical thinking separate themselves from what they
bring under their critical eye and are ready to pronounce
definitive judgments from those lofty heights. This not
only distorts one's view of reality but often leaves the critic
infected by the dire intellectual disease of skepticism. Like
the pitiable person who is unable to trust others and so can
develop no meaningful relationships, the skeptical mind is
unable to trust itself to any tradition of thought or belief
and so can develop no meaningful view of the world. Such
critical thinkers have learned the knack of seeing around
every corner and of pulling apart every thought, belief, and
principle in an endless reductive process by which all is
dissolved in the universal solvent of their skepticism.

The highest quality of the strong mind — that of perceiving the unity of the whole of reality in its constituent parts and of articulating a cosmos of meaning by which to understand and purposively act in the world — has been lost to them. Mistaking an intellectual disease for strength of mind, they become adept at destruction but are incapable of building anything solid. The habit of hyper-criticism then becomes expansionistic and infects the rest of life with its withering presence: relationships with colleagues, attitudes toward the particular institution where one is serving, family life, friendships. The joys of the intellectual life are understandably far from such people.

39. Given our current culture, it is inevitable that those who hold and teach a Christian understanding of reality with clarity and conviction will face opposition. More than ever, Christian professors in our time need to cultivate the intellectual virtues of both love of truth for its own sake and of courage to stand for truth whatever the cost. Opposition to the truth comes in many forms; in the current environment it most often operates subtly. The academy holds out its prizes and its approval for those who do not rock the academic boat in respect to secular assumptions and principles. It is easy enough for Christian professors to avoid unpopular truths without explicitly denying them, going along for the sake of peace. In some societal and strategic contexts that may be exactly the prudent and reasonable stance, but for those whose special charge from God is to pursue truth and to pass it on to young minds, it can also be a disastrous failure. Simply put, the vocation of service to the truth in an age such as ours is not a place of peace but of

conflict. In this respect our time resembles that of the first teachers of Christianity. Saint Paul wrote, "For though we live in the world, we are not carrying on a worldly war, for the weapons of our warfare are not worldly but have divine power to destroy strongholds. We destroy arguments and every proud obstacle to the knowledge of God, and take every thought captive to obey Christ" (2 Cor 10:4-5). Teachers and administrators who are not prepared and willing to engage that conflict — rightly and prudently, with the weapons of warfare provided by Christ — will sooner or later betray their vocation.

The professor as a servant of others

40. Hyper-specialization in the academy has another and more personally devastating effect on those in its grip. It tends to move the professor into a highly individualistic and self-centered mode. We all know how the system works. The way one succeeds in academia is by finding a bit of intellectual turf one can call one's own, becoming expert in it, and then consorting with whatever mini-community is pursuing the same highly specialized interest, as a way of promoting one's career and sustaining a personal corner of the knowledge business. Under this conception, the professor's true identity as a servant of others can easily die through neglect. The primary (and sometimes the only) loyalty expected of the professor is to personal career advancement, with perhaps a secondary loyalty to a small community of like-minded scholars who meet at conferences and exchange one another's articles and books. A bleak loneliness will lie in wait for such persons: hardness of heart toward students, the missed opportunity for one's daily work to transform others and

oneself, the lost chance to join together in the ever-necessary renewal of one's university (the *alma mater* for students) and of the surrounding culture.

41. Current academic culture structurally favors this kind of knowledge business. Research and publishing are valued as career enhancers without much regard for the quality or the importance of the work done, while time spent in preparation for teaching and with students, if occasionally given lip service, is not rewarded and is often viewed as an impediment to career advancement. Such realities as these can hardly be avoided by those in the profession, but the professor will thoughtfully forestall them when possible and will not allow them to become a formative influence. The question the Christian teacher will consistently keep in view is: "Who and what am I serving, and how can I best serve?" The answer to these questions is multiple and may change over time: Christ, of course, then my students, the mission of the particular institution where I am teaching, my colleagues, some portion of the Church, some segment of the society. But the concrete answer to these questions is of fundamental importance.

42. An expression of an individualistic mindset is seen in the way some professors utilize the colleges and universities at which they teach simply to further their own career goals while keeping themselves distant from the institution's mission. Rather than seeing themselves as contributors to a common project as members of a team, academics can tend to chart their own course, "paying their dues" to the host institution while keeping as much time and energy as possible for "my work," for the pursuit of their own personal

interests and goals. This has been an understandable response to the incoherence of the modern secular university. If there is no common mission and no greater good to which one can give oneself, the only sensible thing to do is to work out one's own career path. But the Catholic college or university has, or should have, a clear common mission that transcends the personal career ambitions of any of its faculty or administrators. The professor at such a place looks beyond self to the intellectual, cultural, and moral tradition in which the intellectual vocation is embedded. Not only through professional generosity, but by profound personal devotion to family life and friendships and the Lord (surely, the mature integration of all this within one life is no simple task and takes time), such a scholar grows into an ever-truer incarnation of that deep treasury of wisdom, becoming an icon or window through which the student can see the radiance of the living tradition shining in the lives of its members.

43. By keeping the identity of a servant in the forefront, the Christian professor can also battle against certain potent but ultimately self-absorbed images of the university teacher that can influence the unwary mind: the "Herr Professor" who is looked up to by all because he knows all things, and who speaks a strange academic argot that makes clear the distinction between the intelligent and the stupid; the "Abelard" who is idolized by adoring students and whose cleverness amazes everyone in the room; the "Oxford Don" who wears a tweed jacket, smokes a pipe, and spends long hours in fascinating conversations in pubs; the "Simone de Beauvoir" who is smart and sassy and breaks down outworn conventions while discussing Kafka in a café. Whatever may be true or attractive in these romantic images, they have

self-regard at their center, and they tend to obscure the key question: "Who and what am I serving, right now at this moment?" As is true for all of Christ's servants, the answer should never be: "Myself."

The professor as apostolic missionary.

44. To speak of university teaching as a kind of mission work can seem odd and even out of place. Is this not to confuse different gifts and ways of service? Is the professor to engage in what we usually think of as mission work: preaching, leading Bible studies, engaging in various activities meant to attract people to the faith? Isn't that the point of campus ministry? And who has time for it anyway, given all the teaching, research, and administrative tasks that already dominate life? This kind of response reflects the reduction of our vision of the intellectual task that is so prevalent among us. We tend to think that going to classes and learning is one thing, an objective and often impersonal thing, and growing as a Christian is another, unless we happen to be teaching explicitly theological subjects. But the Christian teacher knows that conversion, something that touches all of a person's powers, is rooted in the renewal of the mind. Learning, even technical learning, is meant to be a growth into the life of Christ "in whom is hid every treasure of wisdom and knowledge" (Col 2:3). We gain knowledge of whatever kind in a moral and spiritual atmosphere that provides a kind of lens for seeing. To understand teaching as a missionary apostolate is to treat learning itself as spiritual activity and the classroom as a place of apostolic mission.

45. The professor at a Catholic university thus looks at teaching as a kind of mission field. Every student is an immortal

soul, and every interaction between professor and student is a communication between one entire spiritual and moral being and another. The Christian teacher does not fall into the debilitating and reductionist error of compartmentalizing humans by setting up zones that supposedly deal with only one aspect of the human. Whether the subject in hand is microeconomics, human anatomy, or history — to say nothing of philosophy or theology — the whole person is present in the professor and the student: mind, will, and spirit. Every student has been made by God for an eternal destiny, and the professor has been given a share in helping others toward that destiny, in however indirect a way. The more the professor cultivates this attitude, the more certain beautiful practices will naturally arise, such as habitually placing study in an overall context of human purpose, noting moral and spiritual questions that naturally arise in the intellectual life, and praying for each student as part of professorial responsibility. Professors who cultivate such attitudes will more naturally be sought out by their students outside class times as well. When the professorial task is understood as an intellectual apostolate, there is no sharp distinction between serving students in or outside of the classroom.

Conclusion

THERE is a BUILT-IN DIFFICULTY whenever one is addressing a situation that has become corrupt and in need of serious reform. By necessity one has to speak of the ways things have gone wrong or have been bent out of their proper shape. But we note what is misshapen only so that we can recognize the right shape. We glance at what has fallen short only to turn the fullness of our gaze upon all things true and good and by that means to approach the One who is Truth and Goodness himself. To be entrusted with the vocation of the Christian professor is to run forward along a road of light and grace. Freed from the deadening shackles of intellectual pride, moved by an ever-deepening insertion into the mind and heart of God, and braced by the high responsibility of preparing other immortal souls for their temporal and eternal destinies, the characteristic note of the Christian teacher, in the midst of lots of hard work, is hope-filled joy. As we continue to grow in the vocation we have received, let that great prayer of Saint Benedict be fulfilled in us: *Ut in Omnibus Glorificetur Deus:* 'May God be glorified in all things!'

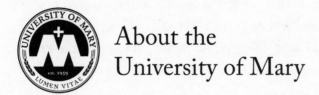

About the University of Mary

The UNIVERSITY of MARY is a private, co-educational Catholic university that welcomes students of all faiths and backgrounds. The university has its origins in the St. Alexius College of Nursing, opened by Benedictine Sisters in 1915. In 1947, these Sisters established Annunciation Priory in Bismarck, a monastic community independent of the original mother-house in St. Joseph, Minnesota. Meanwhile, the nursing college evolved into a two-year women's junior college, and in 1959, the Sisters founded Mary College as a four-year, degree-granting institution. Full university status was achieved in 1986. The University of Mary has been accredited by the Higher Learning Commission of the North Central Association of Colleges and Schools since 1968, and continues under the sponsorship of the Benedictine Sisters of Annunciation Monastery.

Since its beginning, the University of Mary has sought to respond to the needs of people in this region and beyond. Enrollment grew quickly from 69 students to more than 3,800 students today. The university offers more than 50 undergraduate majors, 15 master's degree programs and four doctoral degrees. Classes are conducted at the main campus and other facilities in Bismarck; online; at satellite locations in Arizona, Montana,

Kansas and North Dakota; and at a campus in Rome, Italy.

The University of Mary educates the whole student for a full life, characterized by moral courage and leadership in chosen professions and service to the community. Every aspect of academic and social life is infused with the Benedictine values of community, hospitality, moderation, prayer, respect for persons, and service.

Already one of the most affordable, high-quality private universities in the nation, the University of Mary now offers 'Year-Round Campus,' a unique college-career option that enables students to earn a bachelor's degree in just 2.6 years and a master's degree in four years. This greatly reduces costs and allows students to begin their careers much sooner. The University of Mary offers exceptional educational value, as well as outstanding scholarship and financial aid opportunities. Within six months of graduation, 95 percent of graduates are working or pursuing additional education.

Scholar athletes at the University of Mary participate in 18 varsity sports in NCAA Division II.